A Chair
Keeps the Floor Down

poems by

Susan Dambroff

Finishing Line Press
Georgetown, Kentucky

A Chair Keeps the Floor Down

*For all the children I have taught
and who have taught me*

Copyright © 2021 by Susan Dambroff
ISBN 978-1-64662-454-6 First Edition
All rights reserved under International and Pan-American Copyright Conventions. No part of this book may be reproduced in any manner whatsoever without written permission from the publisher, except in the case of brief quotations embodied in critical articles and reviews.

ACKNOWLEDGMENTS

Thank you to the following publications where these poems have previously appeared, sometimes in slightly different forms:

Conversations with Trees, Finishing Line Press: "Lately"
Stoneboat: "Without Regrets"
Collossus:Home: "A Tender Safety"

Publisher: Leah Huete de Maines
Editor: Christen Kincaid
Cover Art: Lisa Gross
Author Photo: Natalie Strassheim
Cover Design: Natalie Strassheim

Printed in the USA on acid-free paper.
Order online: www.finishinglinepress.com
          also available on amazon.com

               Author inquiries and mail orders:
                      Finishing Line Press
                         P. O. Box 1626
                Georgetown, Kentucky 40324
                            U. S. A.

Table of Contents

Rewired ix

Searching for Home 1
The House Cries 2
Jeffrey Wore a Red Dress 3
Lately 4
Diana 6
Ten Children 7
One Magical Thing 9
The Boy with Coal Black Eyes 10
My Outstretched Arms 12
I Was Not Brave 13
Lockdown 14
Lesson Plans 15
What Feels Like Plenty 16
Without Regrets 19
What's Done Is Done 21
Imprint of Small Hands 24
This Tender Safety 26
No Phone 27
63 28
Retired Teacher 29
At the Public Swimming Pool 30
Tell Me More 31

Rewired

So much I could say
about the way summer comes
in a line of sweet peas
along a country road

about this passage of time
my career ending
all that teaching was
a delightful orchestration
of exchange

but now
I surrender my cobbled mind
to this glade of valley
inexhaustible beauty
in the river's glide

and look for new words
to describe the field
I write in
a thesaurus of new possibility
brings me orbit and scope
circle and space
and calling

I want to make poems
out of the paintings I see
I mutter them out
ambitiously
claim new acquaintances
with frog and salamander
bare feet
welcoming the heat
of rocks

I don't like the word
retired

as it holds within it
some exhaustion
I don't feel

rather choose the word
rewired
as I stare at the
dancing stars of light
on the river's afternoon
where nothing is left behind

and dip into phrases of transparency
glitter and green

Searching for Home

I teach children

> a line is to sit on
> a circle is to hold hands
> red is the color of the door
> that lets you in

Jonathan carries a small photo book
with pictures of abuela, tío, and tía
tu familia I tell him
he pats the slippery pages
home is a drum tapping
like the gate snapping
like his hands in front of his face
fingers flapping
slapping the table
this familiar rhythm
brings him home

> a hand is for reaching
> a mouth is for saying
> a chair keeps the floor down

Jonathan runs to watch the school bus not moving
runs to watch the door open and then close
turning doorknobs he empties one sound into another

The House Cries (1983)

Something the same
about morning
pants at the foot of my bed
socks still stuck in the legs
something the same
about pennies
spilled all over the rug

Something the same
about the news
wars of repetition
Grenada is Lebanon
is Vietnam
is El Salvador
is Nicaragua

Lamar tells me
when his mother
throws the frying pan
the house cries

Somewhere
someone
is killing a child
and calling it
protection

Jeffrey Wore a Red Dress

A boy in my classroom
dresses up in a red dress
because he can turn the skirt
around him
and fly

I am a poet
wearing her dead father's socks
to hold myself down

*

My mother calls
to say her friend Rose
so many states away
can't bring her soup

I read that a town in Tennessee
runs out of money
shuts down the school buses
and children in the mountains
sit on their porches
waiting

*

Thinking there are so many ways
I could die
shopping for underwear
or driving to work

But yesterday
I watched Sofia born
her knees
like blue socks

Lately

my old cat sleeps
in my poems
sleeps beneath her sky blue blanket
in all of my poems
lately
I don't remember my dreams
only that I am forever losing something
worth having
the tree cut
from my window
a sneaker wave
that suddenly
takes me away
lately
I have been craving chocolate
some rush of imagination
I am thigh high
in the unknown
some math without answer
lately I dream autistic children
have long sentences of explanation
I try to read a book in your eyes
lately there is something I want
without asking
like the cat
who gets held
and stroked
and talked to
without asking
lately
I look for myself
in your arms
remember the smell
of what hurt
like parents
who will never come back
from that long drive
across town
lately
I am oceans of fear

the rain that held its breath
for years
and finally fell

Diana

I have always worked with children

I was 13
Diana was 7
she lived next door
her family called her *retarded*

I would walk the thin path
from my house to hers
and her tiny Italian grandma
grey hair in bun
would open the sliding glass door

It was my first job
Diana with black hair swinging
head rolling back and forth
in a figure eight
would make a sideways smile
and take my hand

Ten Children

Jonathan
who counts backwards
only wants the yellow chair
likes monsters

Simon
who loves the written word
wants to repeat the snake's name
says *apple* proudly

Sing
who only likes the color green
runs across the room and says *no running*
takes off her shoe and says *empty*

Leo
who sits right down
but doesn't want to get up again
nods his head, points,
and signs *more*
to make sure he gets the cookie

Billy
who likes little dolls
and calls them *Superman*

Sara
who pretends she's a puppy dog

Travis who has a pillow
in the corner of the classroom
so he can stand on his head

Nathan
who loves the sound of milk cartons
wants to be carried
flirts relentlessly
giggles at bubbles and balloons

Sebastian
who speaks in metaphors

finds the shape of a lamp in everything
draws wine glasses
and the tables they fall off of
says hi to the chair

Da'Rell
who never wants to stop eating
climbs to the top of everything
slaps his knees to the beat
of his name

One Magical Thing

In the café
I hear a woman say
that every night
she asks her children
to say one magical thing
that happened to them that day

They have a map of the world
above the table
with stick pins
to imagine
they might live anywhere

*

At school
Sara tells me to remember her birthday
she says *I'm almost as big as you*
but she can't find the word
that is the number
that is her body
containing her

She buries her feet down deep
in the sand
as if no one can find them

The Boy with Coal Black Eyes

In the middle of the night / I wake
to the boy with coal black eyes

Can I come back to your class?
Can I come back?

What I heard about his teacher / pulling him
up from the floor / by his neck

What I remember / the loose strings
of his body / squirming /grabbing
ricocheting / and how a pile of buttons
pouring through his fingers / could
calm him

Can I come back to your class?

How I pleaded / for the boy with
coal black eyes / that his next class
not be that one

What I reported / about the teacher
forgetting a girl in the grass / eating
dirt / in a neighborhood full of
needles and glass

Can I come back to your class?
Can I?

And what was ignored / the way
the teacher tended to plants / and cut-outs
of hungry caterpillars on the bulletin
board / but not to the children

Can I come back to your class?
Can I come back?

And now / the boy with coal
black eyes / pulled out of class
by his mother / who did her best
to imagine the meaning /of his flapping

hands /may never trust a school
again

And his teacher / on administrative leave
where her story / and the story
of the boy with coal black eyes
may never be / mentioned again.

My Outstretched Arms

Henry oh Henry
in a swing
in a swing

little tight boat
in the waves

*

Henry oh Henry
holds the paper duck
some yellow certainty

his five year old hands
never empty

*

In a dream
my father is alive with open arms
mute little Henry
suddenly has the word for run

*

Henry oh Henry

my outstretched arms
my outstretched arms

I Was Not Brave

On my first teaching job
the boy turning blue
slumped over his wheelchair

Pounding his back
Fingers slid
Through his teeth

*

The time between
the ambulance
and the flowers
his parents brought me
when his color
came back

*

And then
the boy
who didn't

A seizure so small
I hardly noticed

*

As a child
I thought if I prayed
for everyone
they might not
disappear

Lockdown

two teachers / huddled in a closet /children
already gone home / classroom door doesn't
lock / panic over loudspeaker / crouched for
half an hour / without word / of police with
shotguns / men handcuffed on the ground /
I pray *white light (what if) white light (what if)* /
slide the door open / grab the phone / the secretary
says she is sorry / we've been forgotten / didn't get
the signal "All Clear"

*

Today I take to the garden
hummingbird
so close
the absolute beat of her wings
then suddenly gone

This slithering pulse
of life
this vibrant exchange
of color

Lesson Plans

Paint
paper plates yellow
to make the sun

Find everything
that starts with G
gorilla, goldfish, gummy bear

Give out puzzles
as anchors
a duck has a beak
a barn door makes a farm
the alphabet always starts
with the letter A

Teach
like conducting
rows of tumbling chairs

Love the children
as they bite
the ears
off the animal crackers

What Feels Like Plenty

Willy
is afraid of bridges
I talk to him
about imagining them
as candy bars
with cars as tiny ants
moving across them
to find that lightness
in himself
that buoyancy
of safety
his strong bones
holding him up

He wants something
he can control
the wind scares him
he covers himself
with his hood

We talk about kites
and birds
how to feel lifted
and carried

*

Maurice
comes to school
cold and hungry
can't stop his mother
from dying

those mornings
I offer him tea
a cookie to fill

the luxury
of pleasure
the sweetness

*of sugar
in a cup*

*

The children
can't find the words
to tell their stories
can't ground the wires
inside their heads
that keep misfiring

They hold on
to their spots
on the carpet
to the spaces inside
their cubbies
their desks
hide their pencils
grab their favorite crayons
and won't let go

*what feels like enough
what feels like plenty*

*

They hold on
to their food
their clothes
defend the fabric
of their skins

Thomas
whose autistic mind
maps out the world
in predictable lines
needs to know
that the school bus
will always turn right

at the stop sign
any change in direction
will unseat him
he grabs at the driver
and holds on

Elizabeth
with the bluest eyes
drops marbles
into water
to feel the weight
of gravity
she spins and spins
to find her center

Sora
puts her tiny hands
through the openings
of the fence
to pick
yellow mustard flowers
bunches them up
between her fists
and proclaims
that she is taking
them all
home

when we have enough
when we don't run on empty
when there's something left over

Lily
collects sticks
in a pile that gets big enough
to feel like plenty
begins to give them away
on the playground
like presents

Without Regrets

To practice a winter
without regrets
through newscasts
of climate disasters
to remember the remarkable sound
of rain pounding
through long days of work
corralling young children
into loops of captivating play

These children
who in their short lives
have only known drought
I huddle them by the open door
where the rush of wind and rain
catapults onto the playground
where they can't race down the slide
with glee
colliding into each other
with the exalted bump
of doing it again and again

But instead
they witness this
commotion of sky
the rushing surprise of a droplet
spraying against their cheeks

Back in the classroom
two girls take to the easel
dab the brush up and down
all over the page
and call it rain

To remember this
even when the world
is unbearably wounded
like the day a mother
of one of my students
rushes into my classroom
after the San Bernadino shooting

questioning me
about how many ways there are to enter
and exit the room
and what doors are kept locked?

I want to make promises
I can't keep
about saving these tiny children
who after the miraculous downpour
jump into puddles
and watch their footprints
follow behind them

To practice
a winter without regrets
to do the best I can
to show up
to photograph the sunrise
behind a redwood tree
that still stands
in a city of lost homes

And to tell the woman I love
that yes
she should still go to her singing class
even though the bad news
rattles on and on

There is more of a need
than ever
to refuse to belong
to brutality
to covet hope
to put out buckets to save the rain
and to sing

What's Done Is Done

On my last day of teaching
before retirement
I ask the children
as they play
with their favorite cars
or dress up in rainbow capes
or fire hats
Do you want to take that home?
and they drop it
joyfully into the bag
with their name on it

For the last month
I've posted a picture on Facebook
of me in the classroom
counting down the days
gathering children
into sequences of play
making picnics on the floor
doctoring stuffed animals
with band aids and ice

Moments and moments
that will never happen again

*

After the children leave
there is still more to box up
more and more
scurrying to finish

I am ripping and ripping
old reports to shreds—

attendance, goals, progress reports,
all that clicking to save, edit, save
I sign out of my work email
what never seemed done
is done

I leave paperclips and rubber bands
in my desk drawer,
pull sticky notes off the file cabinet—
phone numbers of substitute teachers,
physical therapists, bus drivers,
psychologists, parents
I take what's left of teabags and ceramic mugs,
everything that kept me going—
immune and emotional supports,
oregano oil and rescue remedy
bagged up

I scan the classroom
for what I've forgotten
a painting that once hung
in my daughter's bedroom
a flurry of kites
fly over the landscape
into my arms
to take home

I tell myself
to savor
murals created
with tissue paper butterflies
yellow streaks of a miraculous sun
handprints of affection
everywhere

this flurry of imagination
this field of discovery

*

I was the teacher
opening boxes of surprise
placing pictures
inside thought bubbles
of understanding

I was the conductor and the witness
I was the magician and the mother
and the child I once was
remembering

I am crying in the middle of the classroom
when a colleague takes me in her strong arms

You were the best
Remember, you were the best

Imprint of Small Hands

Retiring from
weeks
years
decades
of work
into a spacious regard
for the first autumn leaves
falling
and the grey tips of time
on my dog's ears

I tame my moods
into simplicity
sketch surprising points
of departure
the elegance of a morning stretch
to a serenading piano
dipping me into pleasure

I move
from the staccato routines
of a job to do
to a cat body
fluidly rounding
into all the layers
yet to bloom

These fresh realms
of discovery
a morning that doesn't rush
to arrive

*

I walk back the days
of readying the classroom
for the perky parade
of children
darting about
across acres of exploration
with a wistful longing

for the richness
and glitter
of those bouncing bodies
wading through puddles
of learning

Their sticky fingers
their butterfly wings
those circles of song and story

Imprints
of their small hands

This Tender Safety

On the bus
I notice the young ones
a child with a stem of grass
in each hand
cuddles in
against grandma's breast

This tender safety
one blade
pulled between her teeth
like a pacifier

This girl
wrapped
between weathered arms
and the gaze
of a kind and mottled face
rocked to sleep
by the ride
of going and stopping

Grandma's hand stroking
the blue stars
on her leggings

One blade of grass falling
from her small hand

No Phone

Today walking the dog
we decide we will only talk about good news
the spray of bougainvillea in the doorway
the cardinal painted on the side of a house
the sign in the window
this block rejects hate
the story of one of your students
going blind
who begins to accept magnification
Taylor Swift's political message
to protect and fight for the human rights we all deserve
that brings in 65,00 voter registrations in a 24 hour period
the mother we pass
cooing at her 2 week old baby
No phone in her hand

63

I'm sparkling and sputtering
into my 63rd year
with labyrinths
of wonder and doubt

Joyful dances on ledges
of realization
glittering trees
and the sweet hibernation
of tulips
bouts of fatigue
stalemates of breath
and wild staccatos of the heart

All membranes of where I've been
mothered and unmothered
fathered and unfathered
witnessed and adored
and left behind
without compass

I stay attentive
to the detailed placement
of words
alchemy of timing and sequence
precise arrangements
of shape and color
blue forget-me-nots blooming
between orange cheeks
of poppies

I join the spontaneous
twirling of children
and remember my own
young surrenders
in fields of buttercups
and welcoming slopes
of freshly fallen snow

Retired Teacher

At the bus stop
the boy
with a blue feather
in his curly black hair
wants to know
why the woman on the sidewalk
doesn't have a leg
Will it grow back?
he asks

I notice the children
their special hats
and fascinations
their daily presence of wonder
eyes widely scanning
to take in more

Why can a lizard grow back its tail?
Why do baby teeth fall out
and grown up teeth replace them?
Why do old teeth fall out
and nothing grows back?

I lean in to this easy spin
of curiosity
first tastes
of the world

Girl with an eager mouth
puckering around
the sweet globe
of a lollipop

At the Public Swimming Pool

We are morning swimmers
who take to the water
as if returning home
its familiar shade of blue

We are
writers and pagans,
lawyers and carpenters,
secretaries and healers,
with our own particular brands
of shampoo

We are
teachers who still teach
and retired ones
who remember
the beat of the classroom
with its adrenaline magic
and fatigue

We tell stories in the shower
of coyotes crossing city streets,
lockdowns at local schools,
the politics of real estate speculators
taking our neighborhoods down

We are homeless women
who are grateful for showers,
renegade artists
who etch fanciful drawings
into the lockers,
we are round and skinny,
firm and rolling
into the folds of time

We are swimmers
who get wet
and then dry together
the certainty of going one way
and coming back the other

Our bold ideas
germinating beneath the water

Tell Me More

As a child
I danced
around the living room
a sparkling
firefly

I loved the story
of Harold and the Purple Crayon
that drew windows
higher and higher
a raising up
that could take me
anywhere

Tell me more

grassy fields
the thrill of buttercups
under my chin
their buttery yellow light

the geography
of pleasure

my first love was a lake
my nickname was Fish
I stroked the speckled backs
of salamanders

Tell me more

Now I am 65
still whirling
through air
and water

bare feet
curving around rocks
to praise the ground

Tell me more

sometimes
there are muddled days
when rising
is just bearing it
a habit
of kitchens and keys
of going out
to come back in
again

Tell me more

sometimes
the balance
falls out of my hips
I want to circle
into a field of bells
find my cat's
meandering
simplicity

there are nights
of strange dreaming
my ancient apple computer
still holds my old poems
filed longings
light my screen

sometimes
I have the taste
of a tired kiss
too many threads of grey
amber eyes
of wanting

Tell me more

I walk beside
sidewalk gardens
each exquisite flower
an imprint of the heart

a piano
wafts out of a window
and the dance
comes back

WITH THANKS TO THE MANY

My deepest gratitude goes to all the children I have taught, for they were the inspiration for this collection of poems. And to their families for the great intimacy of each shared heartache and celebration. A heartfelt thanks to my teaching colleagues and mentors, who helped to shape my career. Amongst them are Cathy Hansen, Barbara Gratta, Jamie Deiner, Diana Solis, Philip Borcover, Kitty Yee, Sharon Piansay, Nancy Lim, Barbara Kalmanson, Pamela Wolfberg, Gwen Wong, Margaret Charnas, Sally Suchmann, Elizabeth Perla, Alexa Malkasian, Deirdre Devine, VoonFee Leow, Stephanie Pass, Kathleen Byrne, Merri Besden, Joe McGovern, Michelle Pereira, Sylvia Weinmann, Isela Cueva Rizzi and Meilani Connolly. And to all the writers who have fueled my imagination and inspired my craft: To Dan Levinson, Kimi Sugioka, Vinnie Peloso, Jennifer Rand, Michael Bickford, Marylee McNeal, Marleen Roggow, and David Tuller for each cut and paste of this manuscript. To my San Francisco Writing Group for the many Saturdays we have spent writing into the mystery together—Jacqueline Berger, Betsy Kassoff, Katherine Lieban, and Laura Horn. To the members of the Lost Coast Writers Retreat who have inspired me under a pavilion of trees. To Eveline Kanes for teaching me about how to make a line spare. To Chris Kammler for the magic of our poetic collaboration. To my dear friends for continuing to show up. And to my partner Janice, and daughter Natalie for the years they have lovingly endured my need for a quiet space to write.

www.ingramcontent.com/pod-product-compliance
Lightning Source LLC
LaVergne TN
LVHW041551070426
835507LV00011B/1039